CW01213129

Original title:
Echoes Under Ice

Copyright © 2024 Creative Arts Management OÜ
All rights reserved.

Author: Gideon Barrett
ISBN HARDBACK: 978-9916-94-510-0
ISBN PAPERBACK: 978-9916-94-511-7

Voices Trapped in the Glacial Hush

In winter's grip, they laugh and shout,
Beneath the freeze, they twist about.
Frosty giggles in the fray,
Making snowmen dance and sway.

Poking fun at penguins bold,
Who'd rather skate than face the cold.
Yet, in their hearts, a warmth they keep,
While all around still falls asleep.

Resonance of the Winter Veil

Beneath the snow, a secret stirs,
As frosty winds hum little purrs.
Silly whispers float like snow,
While igloos chuckle, 'Don't you know?'

The moose wear mittens, what a sight,
And icicles snicker in the light.
With frozen glee, they huddle tight,
In the chilly, shimmering night.

Chilled Reverberations in Time

The polar bears make snowball fights,
While seals applaud from frosty heights.
They spin and twirl on slippery floors,
While snowflakes play on wintry shores.

A frozen choir belts out a tune,
As icebergs sway beneath the moon.
With laughter frozen in mid-air,
Winter's humor sneaks everywhere.

Secrets of the Submerged Realm

Beneath the surface, fish all giggle,
As seaweed fans sway and wiggle.
With icy whispers, they exchange jokes,
While oysters snicker and play like folks.

The starfish roll, the crabs all jive,
In a chilly ball where they arrive.
Bubbles rise with laughter's chime,
As sea creatures dance through the grime.

Palimpsest of Frozen Whispers

In the frost, the voices play,
Sipping tea from yesterday.
Mice in mittens, penguins dance,
Underneath a snowy trance.

A snowman jokes, his carrot grin,
Says, "Let the fun begin!"
With every slip, a laugh is found,
As winter's joy spins all around.

Beneath the Crystal Silence

In icy stillness, giggles hide,
Frogs in scarves do funny slide.
Snowflakes tickle, snowballs fly,
Watch the penguins, oh my, oh my!

Chattering squirrels in a frosty fuss,
Building castles, just for us.
Sledding down the blue-white drifts,
Winter's laugh, the spirit lifts.

Nostalgia in the Chilled Waters

The pond's a mirror, taking bets,
On who will fall, so place your sets!
Silly fish with hats parade,
As winter's chill starts to invade.

But beneath the surface, bubbles rise,
Grinning fishes, they're full of lies!
With a splash, they dance and dart,
Old man winter plays the heart.

Secrets Buried in the Ice

In the ice, a sandwich waits,
Forgotten lunch, oh what fate!
Laughter snores beneath the frost,
Wondering just how much is lost.

A frozen cat, with a frosty stare,
Watch out for those who try to dare!
While snowflakes giggle, twirl and spin,
Lunch will come back, let the fun begin!

Crystals of Forgotten Sounds

A penguin slipped, oh what a sight,
His icy dance brought pure delight.
With frozen fish and slippery glee,
He laughed with seals, quite wild and free.

The whales joined in, a raucous jest,
As bubbles burst, they felt the best.
In a world so cold, they found the fun,
While frosty rays sang to the sun.

Songs of the Silent Depths

Beneath the frost, a mermaid grins,
Tickling fish with playful fins.
Frosty bubbles burst with cheer,
As seaweed twirls, they chime so clear.

A walrus snoozes, dreaming loud,
While crabs compose a marching crowd.
They tap their claws, a rhythmic beat,
In their chilly world, a frozen feat.

Murmurs of the Frigid Abyss

An octopus juggles with a grin,
Snowy flakes that just won't spin.
With tentacles waltzing, they steal the show,
As ice-cold currents begin to flow.

The fish all giggle, swimming fast,
Chasing bubbles, they have a blast.
In this chilly realm, they find their spark,
A frosty fiesta, bright and stark.

Frozen Footsteps in the Silence

A polar bear in a top hat prowls,
Tap-dancing softly while the cold night howls.
His furry friends join in with flair,
As the snowflakes whirl, without a care.

In the stillness, laughter roams,
Creating joy in their frozen homes.
With each tiny step, they giggle loud,
In the winter wonderland, they're quite proud.

Reverberations of the Winter Embrace

In the fridge, I hear a hum,
Frosty whispers, oh so dumb.
Snowflakes flurry, making haste,
A frozen dance that leaves no trace.

Pigeons slide, their feathers fluffed,
Waddling home, they look quite stuffed.
Snowmen giggle, hats askew,
They contemplated quite a brew.

Chilly air fills up my lungs,
Ice cream trucks play silly songs.
Sleds go zooming, kids all scream,
A frosty land, a winter dream.

Beneath the ice, a penguin pranced,
In his tux, he thought he danced.
With each slip, a chuckle gave,
Frosty fun, what a merry rave!

Hushed Verses in the Glacial Still

A snowball fight begins to stir,
From sidewalk cracks, the laughter purrs.
Penguins in shades on icy hills,
They sip hot cocoa, strumming wills.

Thermometers lie, claiming it's free,
While I bundle up, come look at me!
Frosty beards and noses red,
The silliness that lies ahead.

In frozen ponds, ducks skate and glide,
Clumsy flaps, they seem to hide.
With every slip, the laughter bursts,
Ice gives way to winter's thirsts.

Silence reigns with gleeful squeaks,
A frosty tale that each day peaks.
In this chill, we'll find our cheer,
Winter's joke is crystal clear.

Cascading Echoes of the Frigid Flow

Icicles hang with pointy style,
Making snowmen grin and smile.
Nearby, a dog in boots so bright,
Tries to catch snowflakes in flight.

A penguin slides down with a splash,
Spreading joy in a frosty dash.
Snowball projects fly through the air,
Winter's missiles, beware, beware!

Winter frogs hop and croak their tune,
Singing loud beneath the moon.
Bizarre banter, chilly and sweet,
With frozen toes, we wiggle our feet.

Fluffy clouds suspend above,
Snowflakes twist like a winter dove.
In this landscape, we find delight,
Laughter echoes through the night.

The Soundless Dialogue of Ice

In a land where frost seems to speak,
Snowmen whisper, their frosty cheek.
A penguin with a jaunty stride,
Claims the ice is his wild ride.

Sledding down on borrowed tails,
Laughter echoes, breathless wails.
Snowball fights that reign supreme,
Winter folly fuels the dream.

Icicles drip on rooftops' edge,
Tiny drummers, winter's pledge.
As laughter blends with cold crisp air,
We share stories, bold and rare.

Beneath the layer, silence brews,
Whirling snow, our playful muse.
With frosty winks and smiles so coy,
We find the jest in winter's joy.

Ululations of the Frozen Abyss

A penguin skids on crystal floors,
With flippers flapping, chasing doors.
He slips and slides, a frosty sight,
Yelling, "Where's the sun? It's out of sight!"

An otter laughs, performing tricks,
Juggling snowballs, what a mix!
"Catch me if you can!" he roars with glee,
As everyone falls in icy spree.

Fables in the Arctic Shadows

A polar bear with dapper style,
Wears a scarf that's sure to beguile.
Strutting past, he hums a tune,
While seals watch close, they can't immune.

A walrus joins, mustache bold,
Telling stories that never get old.
With laughter booming across the ice,
They all agree, this life is nice!

Beneath the Ice, a Stilled Echo

In caverns deep, where shadows play,
An icefish dreams of dancing all day.
"Oh how I wish I could tap dance bright!"
His fins just flop, no rhythm in sight.

A crab with swagger, he snaps in tune,
"Let's throw a party under the moon!"
But when he tries to move his claws,
He sets off laughter, with rounds of applause!

Sounds of Solitude in the Frost

A snow hare hops, with a wiggle and giggle,
He jumps so high, it's hard not to wiggle!
His ears flop around like they're in a race,
Saying, "Catch me if you can, in this frozen place!"

An arctic fox with a pinch of flair,
Dances on ice, without a care.
With each slip and slide, he howls with mirth,
Declaring, "I rule this frosty earth!"

Songs from the Heart of Winter

In winter's chill, we dance with frost,
Our noses red, like berries tossed.
The snowflakes giggle as they fall,
While penguins waddle, having a ball.

Icicles hang like frozen swords,
While squirrels plot against our hoards.
They peek from holes, those sneaky thieves,
As snowmen sigh and scratch their sleeves.

A snowball fight, a branch takes flight,
Laughter echoes through the night.
We slip and slide on icy trails,
While winter winds tell gliding tales.

So gather 'round the hearth so bright,
With cocoa mugs and tales of fright.
For winter's heart is crackling fun,
In every snowflake, joy's begun.

Memories Buried in Snowbound Dreams

In a blanket white, the world is still,
Yet dreams of summer start to thrill.
A snowman grins, his carrot's a sight,
He hopes for sun, but it's still night.

Buried dreams beneath the snow,
What lies beneath? A slumbering show.
The winter's bite can't freeze our glee,
As squirrels dance in secret spree.

The snow angels giggle, arms stretched out wide,
While pine trees chuckle, their branches beside.
The snowflakes whisper, let's play a game,
While snowmen trade hats, all look the same.

So when you see that winter's grin,
Remember the laughter that lies within.
For buried here among the chill,
Lies warmth and joy, if you just will.

The Lament of the Frozen Waters

On frozen lakes, the fish can't swim,
They sit and ponder, the light grows dim.
With frosty caps, the ducks all quack,
While talking icebergs plot their snack.

A lonely fisherman makes a scene,
With lines and tales, his thirst unseen.
The fish just laugh, they'd rather hide,
Than take the bait from this snowy guide.

The ice creaks low, a silly tune,
As bears breakdance beneath the moon.
A penguin slides into a snow drift,
And with a flurry, gives Mother Nature a lift!

So let us toast this chilly fate,
With fishy jokes that cannot wait.
For laughter warms the floating seas,
And tickles the reeds with winter's breeze.

Hushed Urges Beneath the Surface

Beneath the frost, a hunting spree,
Where beavers scheme in glee-filled glee.
They craft their dams, a treehouse bliss,
While otters play in icy mist.

The quiet whispers of snowflakes small,
As they tease the creatures, one and all.
With wishes made on winter's breath,
They dance around in playful heft.

The foxes giggle, tails in a twist,
While rabbits hop, they can't resist.
Beneath the calm of winter's glare,
Lies mischief brewing, everywhere!

So raise your mugs to winter's charms,
To frozen lakes and snowball arms.
For laughter lies beneath the white,
In every corner, pure delight!

Reflections from a Winter's Grave

A snowman stood with such great pride,
He waved to squirrels as they sighed.
With frosty breath, he told a joke,
But fell apart when the sun broke.

The tombstone said, 'Here lies Fred,'
A frozen smile upon his head.
His friends all laughed, they stomped their feet,
As his carrot nose rolled in the street.

A gust of wind, oh what a thrill,
He twirled around with gleeful chill.
'The winter's cold can't hold me still!'
They danced with joy on yonder hill.

So raise a glass to snowmen bold,
With frosty tales that never get old.
For even in the deepest freeze,
Their laughter floats on every breeze.

Fragments of Time Encased in Ice

A walrus wearing shades so bright,
He slid around in pure delight.
He cracked a grin with a fishy breath,
And claimed he's seen a penguin's death.

In frozen frames, the seals perform,
Tap dancing on a frigid swarm.
Their waddles funny, oh what a sight,
They twirl and spin in the pale moonlight.

A snowflake fell with graceful flair,
And whispered secrets to the air.
'I'm just a bit too cold to stay,'
As it melted slowly, slipped away.

But laughter rings from icy halls,
Where time stands still and something falls.
For in each flake, a giggle lies,
A frozen joke beneath bright skies.

Invitations from the Depths

A fish in shades sent out invites,
To all his friends for chilly nights.
With bubbles rising, they would cheer,
As snowflakes fell to bring them near.

The octopus, with eight long arms,
Twirled in the depths, displaying charms.
He juggled ice, a juggling feat,
While all the other critters beat their feet.

A lobster danced in shiny shoes,
Proclaimed a ball with colorful news.
He snapped his claws, they went "Ka-Pow!"
As crabby friends grumbled, "Here we go now!"

So raise your fins and claws up high,
Invitations sent beneath the sky.
For winter's chill brings friends anew,
With laughter echoing, frosty and true.

The Sighs of Cold Shadows

In shadows lurked a wheezy ghost,
Who sneezed so loud, he scared his host.
'Excuse my chill,' he said with glee,
'It's not my fault if you can't see!'

A shadow danced with floppy glee,
While chuckling at the grassy spree.
'Why must the sun disrupt my play?
I'm only here to joke and sway!'

The cold winds sighed, they didn't care,
As giggles traveled through the air.
'We're just the ghosts of frosty nights,
Who love to share fantastic sights!'

So come and play in gleeful arms,
Where chilly laughs bring hearty charms.
For in the shadows, fun is found,
As whispers dance and laughter bounds.

Echoes of Time in the Frigid Expanse

In the depths where snowflakes drift,
Ancient yodels give a lift.
Frosty murmurs, quite absurd,
Silly whispers, never heard.

Chilly giggles fill the air,
Penguins dance without a care.
Chattering teeth make jokes so grand,
In this frosty wonderland.

Frozen laughter, out of breath,
Tickling toes—it's life and death!
Slippery floors cause slips and falls,
Frozen jokes... oh, how it sprawls!

Ice-skate pranks go on and on,
While snowmen play a funny con.
Witty banter in the chill,
Creating joy—it's quite a thrill!

Melodies Ensnared by the Cold

In the winter's frosty grip,
Frozen tunes cause quite a blip.
Hummingbirds take icy flights,
Fluttering 'round, oh what a sight!

Snowflakes twirl like ballerinas,
While polar bears serve up subpoenas.
Chilly choirs sing off-key,
Echoing giggles, full of glee.

Memory bells are made of glass,
Joking squirrels try to pass.
Frosty laughter fills the night,
With each jingle, spirits bright.

Gleeful chimes on every street,
Silly snowmen dance their feet.
Winter's fun, wrapped up tight,
In this cool, comedic light!

Wraiths of Sound in the Icy Stillness

Frosty apparitions float about,
Making goofy sounds, no doubt.
Whispers chilling down the lane,
Ghostly giggles—what a pain!

Frostbitten jokes from hidden souls,
Tales of mischief fill the holes.
Windy puns swirl without a care,
Tickling frost on the chilly air.

Ghoulish grins in the frozen light,
Making fun of winter's bite.
Chattering teeth join the fun,
While snowflakes dance and take a run!

In the stillness, jokes unfold,
Wraiths of laughter, brave and bold.
Frosty fun, a crazy mix,
In this chilly world of tricks!

Cold Currents of Hidden Memories

Beneath the ice, forgotten jokes,
Playful pranks from silly folks.
Frozen tales of old-time cheer,
Echo through the atmosphere.

Windswept stories, sharp as ice,
Charming smiles, oh, what a slice!
Hilarious whispers in the freeze,
Warm hearts wrapped in chilly ease.

Muffled laughter, crisp and clear,
Bouncing back, while we all cheer.
Silly fish with funny faces,
Join the fun in all the spaces.

Warmed by memories, strong and tight,
In the frosty glow of night.
Cold currents of fun, oh divine,
In this winter wonder—a happy line!

Chilling Murmurs of the Deep

Beneath the frost, they tell a joke,
A seal slips by with a slippery poke.
The fish all giggle, swim in a line,
While penguins dance, looking quite divine.

A whale makes bubbles, sings quite off-key,
The octopus laughs, 'Oh, that's just me!'
They've got no shame in this icy place,
Cracking up as they glide with grace.

Polar bears chuckle on frozen sheets,
While walruses clap in their cozy seats.
With every chill, a laugh we hear,
In the deep, the chill's full of cheer.

So if you dive deep 'neath the frozen sea,
Join in the fun, let your worries flee.
For laughter lingers in the cold delight,
In the silence, it sparkles, oh so bright.

Lost Sonatas in the Icebound Silence

A piano's lost under layers so thick,
With keys made of ice, it plays quite a trick.
A polar bear tries to hit a few notes,
But all that comes out are frosty anecdotes.

The snowflakes dance to a symphony cool,
While fish in tuxedos play by the pool.
Clams are the critics, they clap their shells,
Creating a ruckus with hearty yells.

In the stillness, the melody sways,
As seals join in with their vocal displays.
It's a concert of whimsy, all frozen in time,
With tunes of the frigid, oh so sublime.

Yet as they perform, the ice cracks a grin,
And laughter erupts from deep within.
For even in silence, the joy we find,
Is the music of laughter, cold winds intertwined.

Tides of Frosted Echoes

Waves of giggles beneath the white tide,
Crabs wearing hats, oh, what a wild ride!
A flounder with shades, claims he's the star,
While jellyfish bob, playing air guitar.

On icebergs, seals stage a comedy show,
With punchlines delivered by caught-in-a-whoa!
As snow drifts witness, they roll on the floor,
Winter's a laugh fest with something in store.

The narwhals trumpet with silly surprise,
As freezing winds play pranks under blue skies.
A frozen ballet, the fish start to twirl,
In a dance of the frosty, every flap a whirl.

So come for a swim, just bring your best grin,
In these chilly waters, laughter's the win.
For tides of fun flow through each chilly glance,
Making winter's frosty heart want to dance.

Faint Refrains from the Abyss

In the depths where it's dark as coal,
A sea cucumber jokes, "I'm on a roll!"
With whispers bubbling from bubbles and foam,
A crab courts a dolphin, calling it home.

"Why so blue?" asks a fish with a cap,
"Because I dream of a sunbathing nap!"
In the gloom, the chatter softly bounces,
As starfish snicker and silly sea sponges.

Anemones sway to the tales of old,
Of mermaids with hiccups and treasures of gold.
The octopus jests, "I'm multi-tasking here!
Juggling my thoughts while I shed a tear."

But through the giggles and watery jest,
A truth remains, laughter's the best.
In every dark corner from which we might hide,
There's fun to be found, with friends by our side.

Haunting Lullabies of the Deep

In a sea where fish sing silly tunes,
A whale once danced, beneath the moons.
Octopuses paint with their ink so bright,
While seals are napping, what a sight!

A mermaid hummed a jolly jig,
While starfish winked, feeling quite big.
Suddenly, a crab joined the play,
Pinching his friends in a comical way.

The jellyfish laughed as they floated by,
Telling fish tales that made them cry.
Fishes rolled over in a bubbly glee,
Wishing to join in the undersea spree.

But when the sun sets, it all goes still,
The playful crew down there, what a thrill!
Lullabies haunt as night starts to creep,
While all the fishy folks drift off to sleep.

Melodies Lost in the Snow

A snowman strummed on a carrot guitar,
While penguins danced, oh so bizarre.
The winter winds carried a frosty tune,
As rabbits hopped by, one in a costume.

The polar bears spun, their fur a-white,
Chasing after snowflakes that twinkled bright.
With snowballs thrown in a merry melee,
They stumbled and tumbled, what a display.

A Christmas tree stood, adorned with cheer,
As squirrels threw acorns, oh dear, oh dear!
It's dance-off time in this frosty land,
Even ice skates joined, holding fluffy hands.

Yet under the snow, a secret lies,
Where snowflakes giggle, the softest sighs.
Melodies lost, yet oh, so profound,
In the winter's embrace, joy can be found.

The Sound of Shattered Stillness

The mountain quiet, like a sleepy log,
Then suddenly bursts with a croaky frog.
His friends all jump for a hefty cheer,
Shattering silence, spreading good cheer.

Sled dogs barking in a tangled heap,
Chasing the echoes that jump and leap.
A snowball rolled, tumbling with glee,
Knocking down penguins as silly as can be.

The icicles drip like a dripping tap,
While rabbits perform their best acrobat.
Winter's laughter, a sound most loud,
As critters frolic, all joyous and proud.

Yet when night falls, all comes to rest,
In cozy burrows, they banter their best.
The sound recedes, but never quite goes,
In the heart of the chill, pure joy always flows.

Beneath the Icebound Surface

Beneath the layer of frosted glass,
A fish serenades with a bit of sass.
He wiggles and squirms for a captive crowd,
Making them laugh, oh joy, so loud!

A seal popped up with a playful grin,
Joining the fun with a bubbly spin.
Tiny snowflakes join the quirky dance,
In the grand show where all take a chance.

But lurking below, a crab with flair,
Attempts a dance that's quite rare.
With a pinch and a twist, he steals the show,
As laughter rings out in the chilly flow.

So if you're out on the frozen spree,
Listen close to the underwater glee.
For what lies below, both silly and nice,
Is a world full of fun beneath the ice.

Pulse of the Glacial Heart

In the depths where penguins prance,
And polar bears do a funny dance,
Chill vibes flow through icy lanes,
As snowflakes laugh, no one complains.

A frosty world, absurdly bright,
Snowmen gossip late at night,
With carrot noses all askew,
They munch on ice cream, who knew?

Glacial hearts beat, tick tock, tick,
While icebergs waltz, oh what a trick,
A frozen party, come and see,
Where frost and fun hang out for free.

So let the winter winds blow wild,
As frosty creatures play and smile,
Beneath the chill, there's warmth to find,
In silly jests that freeze the mind.

Secrets Carried by the Winter Wind

Whispers ride on chilly gales,
As snowflakes tell their silly tales,
The trees all chuckle, branches sway,
While icy critters slide and play.

In glimmering caves, the secrets spin,
Where snowmen tell of winter's win,
An igloo dance, a snowball fight,
A frozen feast, what pure delight!

With every gust, laughter grows,
Across the frost, the humor flows,
Witty winds through spindrift glide,
As we all join the frosty ride.

So hold your mittens, grab a chair,
And join the chill in winter's air,
For secrets carried through the night,
Bring giggles wrapped in pure delight.

The Silent Choir of Frozen Echoes

In a world where silence sings,
The chilly choir of winter flings,
A symphony of ice and cheer,
With frosty notes that tickle ear.

Snowflakes whisper, "What a scene!"
As snowmen join, all dressed in green,
With carrot ties and frosty grins,
They harmonize, the fun begins!

This silent choir, a quirky bunch,
Makes winter's joy the best to munch,
As hoarfrost twirls in giddy glee,
Encouraging laughs, wild and free.

So let the frozen world unite,
In laughter bright, oh what a sight,
For every note a wintery jest,
In icy realms, we find our best.

Murmuring Depths of the Frozen Dance

Deep below, the ice does sway,
As fish perform their ballet play,
A cavorting crew, all scales and fins,
In winter's grip, where fun begins.

Beneath the frost, the secrets twirl,
In icy depths, the bubbles whirl,
A dance of life, both sly and spry,
As penguins watch and giggle by.

With glacial grooves and chilly beats,
The depths awake with frosty fleets,
While seals in tuxedos prance about,
Wordless laughter, no need to shout!

In this realm where fun takes flight,
The frozen dance ignites the night,
So join the merry depths so bright,
And let your heart take joyful flight.

The Hushed Symphony of Ice

When winter's chill takes to the stage,
A penguin slips, ready to engage.
He tries to dance but falls with flair,
The snowflakes giggle, floating in the air.

The frostbound trees all start to sway,
In rhythmic shivers, they joke and play.
A snowman chuckles, hat askew,
His carrot nose says, "What's wrong with you?"

Icicles hang like droll chandeliers,
They clink and clatter through the years.
As frosty winds begin to hum,
They tease the squirrels, 'Hey, what's your sum?'

Beneath the surface, laughter flows,
But only fish know how it goes.
They wiggle and giggle beneath the sheet,
While ice skates glide with silly feet.

Muffled Voices from Below the Frost

Beneath the surface, fish do meet,
Trading jokes in a chilly suite.
"Why the long fins?" one fish will cry,
"To keep up with all the salmon spry!"

Snowflakes whisper in a numbed delight,
While frosty critters plan to unite.
The groundhog's pranks always draw the laughs,
Snap a selfie with the snow-covered staffs!

Ninety penguins waddle for fun,
Racing on ice, they think they're the one.
But they slip and slide, who wins the race?
"Was that a tumble, or a snowball's embrace?"

A muffled sound from the frozen deep,
"Who's got my hat?" one fish will peep.
Jokes bounce around in the still, cold air,
The laughter of winter, everywhere!

Imprints of Sound in the Cold Night

In the cold night, sounds echo shy,
A muffled 'thump' of a snowball fly.
The owls hoot, they're feeling bright,
As snowflakes twirl, a dazzling sight.

Beneath the chill, laughter lays low,
A bear in a hat? Oh, don't you know!
His big paws swipe, trying to catch,
A snowball flurry, oh what a match!

Crickets chirp through the frost-bit air,
While rabbits leap, without a care.
They whisper tales of the frozen spree,
As stars above giggle, 'Oh, let it be!'

Muffled giggles from the winter's heart,
Wonders of sound, an icy art.
The moon winks down at the snowmen crew,
Their funny shape, quite the view!

Lament of the Ice-Covered Void

The void is silent, but has its cheer,
A snowman weeps, 'Oh, where's my beer?'
With frosty tears that sparkle bright,
He's missing laughs on a wintry night.

The snow drifts sigh, they twist and tease,
While winter's chill brings hardly a breeze.
A squirrel shouts up to the sky,
"What happened to spring? Don't make me cry!"

Polar bears lounge, looking perplexed,
With ice-covered jokes just left unvexed.
They chuckle softly, behind their paws,
"In the fridge, we're stuck – let's take a pause!"

And so the winter hums its tune,
A softer giggle, like a sleepy moon.
For laughter lives in the ice's embrace,
In the void, it's fun – a frosty space!

Beacons in the Winter Gloom

A penguin slipped on frozen ground,
He flapped his wings, but fell, not found.
The seals all laughed, what a sight to see,
As snowflakes rained on his wild spree.

The polar bear danced with clumsy grace,
Spinning and twirling, what a funny place.
His furry friends gathered round in cheer,
While he shook off snow like a big blonde deer.

Frosty the snowman lost his hat,
With a gust of wind, oh what of that!
He wobbled and bobbled, then started to roll,
Into the field, oh dear, what a stroll!

So cheers to the winter, so bright and fun,
With giggles and grins, we race 'til we're done.
In the cozy of chilly, let laughter ignite,
Our frosty escapades bring joy through the night.

Harmonies Through the Crystal Veil

A marmot plays on a frozen log,
Singing his heart out, like a little cog.
While snowflakes twirl, it's a wintry groove,
He twitches his nose, and starts to move.

Chilly winds whistle, they join in the song,
The trees sway and sway, but something feels wrong.
A squirrel popped out, wearing a scarf,
"Why are we singing? It's a bit too harsh!"

With playful notes, the icicles gleamed,
As a rabbit hopped in, but quickly he dreamed.
Of warm summer days and carrots galore,
Then woke with a start, back to ice—and more!

So let's sing together, in this wintery zone,
With laughter and joy, never alone.
In this land of snow, where the funny was made,
Let's dance through the frost, in a whimsical parade.

Whispers Beneath the Frost

Beneath the frost, where secrets lie,
A turkey strutted with no reason why.
He slipped on ice and flew like a kite,
"Whoops! I was going to take a flight!"

The owls giggled from their cedar tree,
"Is it winter or just your clumsiness spree?"
As his feathers fluffed like a big snow cloud,
He shrugged off laughter, feeling quite proud.

The snowflakes twirled in silly delight,
As a turtle waddled, oh what a sight!
A slow-motion flip, she spun on her shell,
While nature chuckled, wishing her well.

So gather the critters, let's share a cheer,
For wintertime antics, spreading good cheer.
In the chill of the night, with chuckles we've tossed,
There's laughter to find, even beneath the frost.

Shadows Beneath the Surface

In frigid depths, a fish took a dive,
With a splash and a splash, it was quite the vibe.
But who would have known, with a flip of a fin,
He'd land on a seal with a very loud grin?

"Did you catch that wave? It was one for the books!
You moved like a dolphin, with some funny looks."
The seal rolled over, saying with glee,
"Just trying to snag a friend for tea!"

The shadows swirled as a walrus squeezed through,
With blubber and charm, saying, "I'll greet you!"
"Join us for games, we can play all night,
Winter's a party, we'll feast with delight!"

As darkness fell, and stars twinkled bright,
Under the surface, our laughter took flight.
In the realms of winter, where fun's the whole deal,
Let's dance through the night with a whir and a squeal.

Cold Murmurs of the Ocean Floor

Bubbles swagger, making noise,
A fish jokes while he plays with toys.
Seaweed sways, a dance so slick,
Starfish laugh, oh what a trick!

Crabs wear hats and prance around,
Mollusks giggle, a squeaky sound.
The octopus has quite the flair,
Telling tales with ink in the air.

The deep blue, a comedy show,
In frosty realms where laughter flows.
Mermaids snicker, their hair a mess,
As icebergs juggle in their dress.

Waves tickle turtles, what a sight,
While seals slide with sheer delight.
Gelid gags in the ocean's glow,
Make the salty critters steal the show!

Lyrical Hush of the Shimmering Ice

Up above, the snowflakes sway,
While penguins groove in a wobbly ballet.
Crystals hum, a glimmering tune,
As frosty breezes serenade the moon.

In frozen lands, the laughter rings,
Polar bears wear crowns made of springs.
The walruses dance with graceful might,
In a wintery ball, they twirl so light.

A snowman cracks a silly grin,
While frosty friends break out in spin.
The chill is cool, the jokes sublime,
Winter gigs are just in time!

Icicles dangle, with a wink and a nod,
As snowflakes chuckle at their frosty odds.
In this icy scene, joy takes flight,
With shimmering laughs from day to night!

The Stillness Beneath the Frozen Depths

Under layers of icy sheen,
Where creatures plot with mischief keen.
A squid slips on a glacier's edge,
As a seal dances, making a pledge.

Platters of ice enhance the fun,
While penguins chuckle, a frosty run.
Underwater, a laughter blend,
In chill and thrill, the good vibes send.

Fish tell tales of wacky dreams,
With shimmering scales, they plot their schemes.
Ancreatures joke, as bubbles rise,
In silent depths, its laughter flies.

Winter's canvas, a comic sight,
Laughter ripples, pure delight.
Beneath the chill, joy leaps and twirls,
In the depths where humor unfurls!

Silence Wrapped in Winter's Cloak

Under snow, a hush prevails,
As critters chuckle at frozen tales.
The air is crisp, the mood is bright,
While laughter echoes through the night.

Squirrels in sweaters take a peek,
While snowflakes crash with ticklish squeak.
They build bold forts and dodge the chill,
As winter's gags bring endless thrill.

Frosty friends on sleds so wide,
Zoom down slopes, with giggles that slide.
The trees do sway, in playful trance,
As they join in on this winter dance.

Beneath the cloak of winter's grace,
A joyous chaos finds its place.
In this serene, enchanting show,
Laughter wrapped tight, as breezes blow!

Voices from the Chilled Abyss

In winter's grip, the penguins plot,
With snowball fights, they give it a shot.
They waddle and slip, with flippers in play,
Chasing their tails till the end of the day.

Beneath the frost, a turtle sneezes,
A shout of laughter; the ice shard freezes.
The fish swim by with a curious glance,
Wondering what made the chilly ones dance.

Frogs in mittens sing a cool tune,
While the ice melts faster than we can swoon.
Silly snowmen start to loose their hats,
As the squirrels race by in their furry spats.

With giggles stuffed in snowman's nose,
The icy world hosts jokes nobody knows.
In this frozen land with warmth profound,
Laughter rings loud, with no one around.

Secrets Wrapped in Winter's Embrace

A polar bear sneezes, the tale's never done,
Caught in the storm, he thinks it's all fun.
He's juggling icicles, a sight to behold,
While laughing at seals, who are trembling and cold.

Snowflakes whisper, secrets away fly,
A moose wearing earmuffs waves bye-bye.
The rabbits hop, dressed as ice queens and kings,
Playing hopscotch on patches of frosty flings.

The owl's a comedian, wisecracks abound,
He jokes with the snow, what a funny sound.
Squirrels chuckle at the frost from above,
Creating a mischief that's wrapped in warm love.

Under the twilight, secrets unfold,
Warm laughs spin stories that never grow old.
In winter's embrace, fun flickers and glows,
A tapestry woven with friendships that grow.

Reverberations in the Frigid Stillness

In the blizzard's roar, a snowman stands tall,
With a carrot for a nose, he's having a ball.
Winds blow the jokes past the icy trees,
While snowflakes giggle in the winter breeze.

A polar bear shuffles, clumsy yet proud,
Swaying in rhythm, not drawing a crowd.
He thinks he can dance on a patch of slick ice,
But his flippers keep slipping - oh, isn't it nice?

With frosty cheers, the animals gather,
To share their tales and jitter with laughter.
Snowflakes flutter like giggling confetti,
In the stillness, there's joy – oh, so ready!

The twinkle of stars adds to the joke,
As snowmen wobble, it's a sight to provoke.
In the quiet of night, fun takes its flight,
With chuckles and hoots, they'll dance till the light.

Shadows Beneath the Glacial Surface

In the dim of the ice, a shadow appears,
A fish wearing glasses and cracking up cheers.
He swims with the shrimp, making puns on their tails,
While laughter erupts from the cold, icy gales.

A walrus slides down an icy big hill,
Tumbling and spinning - oh what a thrill!
He yells to the seals, "Come join in the fun!"
And suddenly they're juggling, a playful run!

With lollipops made of frozen blue rays,
The critters beneath play in silly ways.
An octopus humorously shows off his socks,
As they dance in the waves of the icy cold blocks.

So here in the chill, the fun's far from sparse,
In shadows they giggle, with humor so sparse.
In a land made of winter, delight we embrace,
With laughter like snowflakes, a warm-hearted space.

Songs of the Icy Dawn

In the chill of the morning light,
Snowflakes dance, oh what a sight!
Squirrels slip on icy roofs,
Chasing their tails, in frozen goofs.

The coffee pot hums a frostbit tune,
As penguins in bow ties waddle by soon.
With each slip and slide, laughter ensues,
Who knew ice could cause such amusing blues?

Mittens lost, in the snowy fray,
Snowmen sporting hats that sway.
A chilly breeze brings cheeky grins,
To the frosty party, the fun begins!

Winter's stage, where antics abound,
Clumsy critters all around.
A flurry of laughs as we all rejoice,
In the icy dawn, we find our voice!

Murmurs from Below the Frosted Veil

Underneath the frosty crust,
Fish make jokes, oh how they lust!
With gills that twitch and fins that flare,
They plot a dance without a care.

A walrus dons a sash and tie,
With a laugh that echoes through the sky.
The narwhals join in a chorus keen,
Singing tunes of the ocean's sheen.

Icebergs wobble, no need to rush,
As seals perform the fanciest hush.
Wrapped in blankets, they create a scene,
Frolicking fun, no need for green!

A float of whimsy on the tide,
Through chilly waters, they take pride.
With winter's chill, so warm and bright,
Beneath the veil, they dance with delight.

The Serene Silence of Frozen Depths

Deep in the ice where all is calm,
There's a clown fish, pure and balmy.
He's telling tales of bubbles galore,
With giggles that echo from the ocean floor.

Octopus dressed in a top hat grand,
Shrinks his leg while making a stand.
He juggles pearls with graceful flair,
As sea turtles wink, an ocean affair.

Unicorns of the deep spread joy,
While jellyfish float, a silly ploy.
In serene silence, the laughter flows,
Like a frozen stream where everything glows.

Bubbles rise, bursting with glee,
A banquet of marine jubilee.
In this frosty realm under the waves,
The depths are alive with splashes and raves!

Hidden Harmonies in the Cold

In frozen woods, where critters play,
Chirps and squeaks lead the ballet.
Bunnies hop to a frosty beat,
While mischievous foxes dance on their feet.

Under the boughs, secrets dwell,
A choir of owls sings, oh so well!
With each hoot, a giggle spreads,
As snowflakes twirl and winter treads.

The trees sway softly to the tune,
Of winter nights and a silvery moon.
Nature's laughter rings through the air,
With every flake, joy to declare!

In hidden corners, harmony reigns,
With every chuckle, the ice refrains.
Come join the fun beneath the cold,
In a world of laughter, treasures unfold!

Shivers of the Hidden Currents

Beneath the frost, a tickle glows,
As fish in jackets strike ridiculous poses.
They waddle like penguins, all dressed so neat,
While bobbing for snacks, they tumble and cheat.

The bubbles giggle, oh what a sight,
They dance in the deep, lost in icy delight.
With each frosty breath, they chatter and sway,
Rehearsing their jokes 'til the end of the day.

Polar bears chuckle, can't help but grin,
Watching the seal, as they slip and they spin.
"Oh what a party!" the belugas all cheer,
"To be this absurd in our wintery sphere!"

So next time it freezes, and nature's all bright,
Remember the fun that happens at night.
For laughter can glide and swim in the freeze,
Where the coolest of creatures bring all to their knees.

Voices of the Winter Refuge

In frosty caves, the shadows croon,
A chorus of critters, beneath the pale moon.
With flippers and fins, they gather and sing,
"A walrus with style, let's give him a ring!"

The snowflakes whisper, in spirals they swirl,
While otters in top hats perform a great twirl.
They juggle with snacks, well, fish, of course,
As laughter erupts from the whole of the source.

The crystal-blue water holds secrets, it seems,
Of ticklish tales shared in deep winter dreams.
With giggles and splashes, a splash of delight,
They revel in antics 'til out goes the light.

So if you dive down where the frosty fun lies,
You might find a party in a snow-covered guise.
A raucous reminder that warmth can still thrive,
Even under the cold, we're all still alive!

Echoes from the Abyssal Veil

Down where the sun can't tickle your toes,
Resides a party where anything goes.
Squids wear top hats, and tuna play drums,
While icicles giggle and bubble like gums.

The lobsters are laughing, in crabs' salty jokes,
As whales hum along in their fantastic cloaks.
The seaweed wags, oh so sprightly it seems,
While dolphins flip high in the best of schemes.

A narwhal with flair boasts the best frozen tricks,
Flipping through bubbles with acrobatic kicks.
"Come join our gala!" the seals all implore,
With fishy confetti that falls from the floor.

So if you wander where the currents all play,
Remember those laughs that float far away.
For even down deep, with the cold all around,
Joy hides in the depths, where pure fun can be found.

Translucent Whispers Beneath the Ice

Beneath the chill where shadows convene,
A world full of giggles springs bright from the keen.
The frosty ducks quack in a tune that's all wrong,
As icicles tinkle, joining right in the song.

The owls take bets on the fish's next leap,
With sips of cold cocoa, a frosty little steep.
They plan up some pranks for the seals in disguise,
While snowflakes drop in, like unwelcome spies.

The polar bears lounge, tossing snacks left and right,
Pointing and laughing at all of the sight.
Hearts warmed by the fun, though the air's icy spray,
A heartier winter than warm summers play.

So when you think winter is cold and it's dreary,
Remember the laughter that makes it so cheery.
For underneath frost, where the wild antics flow,
Is a folly-filled winter that puts on a show.

Whispers of the Neptunian Night

The fish wear tuxedos, quite a sight,
They dance through the kelp in the pale moonlight.
"Mind the bubbles!" they giggle and swirl,
As seaweed sways like a party girl.

An octopus juggles his dinner plate,
While seahorses gossip, they just can't wait.
"Did you see the crab in that silly hat?"
"I heard he tried salsa, can you imagine that?"

A chorus of clams click their shells in glee,
As starfish cheer up their dull party spree.
"More plankton, please!" yells a clam with zest,
"And let's dance till dawn, we're not getting rest!"

Through shimmering currents, the laughter flows,
In deep-sea thrills where nobody knows.
Tonight's all about the wacky and bright,
As laughter rings out through the Neptunian night.

Chilled Voices Beneath the Surface

The icy depths hum a frosty tune,
Where fish play cards under the pale blue moon.
"Who shuffled the kelp?" yells a grumpy trout,
"I swear, this game's rigged, I'm almost out!"

A walrus croons in a baritone squall,
While penguins tap dance, they slip and fall.
"Watch out for the ice!" they laugh with delight,
As seals join the chorus, a slippery sight.

From under the frost, laughter breaks free,
A holiday party for fish, can't you see?
"Pass the sea cucumber!" cries one in glee,
"Let's toast to the dolphins — they play so free!"

In bubbles and giggles, the currents confide,
While snowflakes fall down like confetti wide.
Chilled voices and nonsense fill all the nooks,
As nature's own joke book gets plenty of looks!

The Unseen Choir of the Deep

In the shadows, a whale strikes a note,
While jellyfish jam like they're on a boat.
"Do you hear that bass?" asks a blushing shrimp,
"It's a symphony grand, or a big fish's blimp!"

The coral rocks out, sprouting some tunes,
As clownfish joke like absurd little loons.
"Let's blow bubbles in harmony, let's have a ball,
With tunes from the deep, we invite one and all!"

Anemones sway with a rhythm so fine,
While sea cucumbers groove in a line.
"Who wants to join us in this dance of delight?"
Bubbles erupt, but all ends up right.

Underwater laughter, all silly and bright,
From creatures unseen, they gather for night.
The unseen choir croons songs full of cheer,
As the ocean shimmers, inviting all near.

Melodies Lost in Frozen Dreams

Beneath fragile layers, the music does play,
With walruses winking and bears on display.
"I can't believe we're chilling like this!"
"Let's make a snowman, with a frosty kiss!"

Pufferfish giggle, puffed with glee,
While a narwhal thinks he's a sight to see.
"Is that a horn or just an old broom?"
They laugh and they twirl in their snowy room.

Melodic echoes drift through the frost,
As snowflakes perform, they never get lost.
"Bring on the ice cream!" a sealjoyfully cries,
While dolphins swoon under bright candy skies.

Beneath every layer, fun lies in wait,
With laughter bubblewraping this cold, icy fate.
In frozen dreams, melodies hold their reign,
Where silly serenades dance in the main.

Chants of the Frosted Depths

In the depths where bubbles tickle,
The fish wear hats, oh what a pickle!
They wiggle and dance, with grins so wide,
As snowflakes play hide and seek with pride.

An octopus juggles cold silver bombs,
While penguins slide down in stylish uniforms.
With frosty jokes that make you guffaw,
Even walruses chuckle, 'What a flaw!'

Beneath the chill, a party does brew,
An arctic rave with an icy crew.
They toast with snowballs, such frosty cheer,
With laughter that rings from far and near.

So if you dive down, take care, be spry,
For in frozen depths, the fun's way too sly.
With every bubble and tickling frost,
You'll lose your stern, have fun at all cost!

Icebound Whispers of the Spirit

Beyond the chill, the spirits giggle,
As frostbitten winds play a cute little jiggle.
They whisper secrets in a cold ballet,
Trying to trick the night as it plays.

A polar bear in a tutu prances,
With comedic flair, he takes his chances.
While seals in snorkels float side to side,
Making waves with laughter, teal, and wide.

The ghosts swirl around, in breathy tone,
As snowmen joke, 'Hey, we're not alone!'
With carrot noses pointing at stars,
While yetis canoodle in old rusty cars.

So listen close, to antics of lore,
In the frosty air, there's laughter galore.
The spirits call with a giggling sigh,
'Take life lightly, let your troubles fly!'

Traces of Light in the Arctic Dark

In the dark where shadows play tag,
A moose in pajamas shows off his swag.
With twinkling lights of the aurora as flair,
He dances with grace in the cold, frosty air.

The igloos echo with muffled laughter,
While snowflakes dance as if chasing after.
A yeti asks, "Do I look okay?"
As he spins in a whirlwind, hip-hip-hooray!

Little critters play hide and go seek,
In frosty nooks, with tails that peek.
They giggle and chatter, all in delight,
The chilly fun lasts far into the night.

So if you find yourself lost in the shimmer,
Join in the laughter, let your heart glimmer.
For in this world of ice and glow,
The funny times keep rolling, don't ya know?

Distant Calls from the Polar Night

From the blue dark, a seal starts to sing,
In a croaky voice, 'Oh, winter's my king!'
The walruses laugh, with tusks as their props,
Belly flopping around, like pancake drops.

A hare in snow boots hops, oh so spry,
"Why wear two? One's for style, that's why!"
With icicles dangling like chandeliers,
They throw snowballs, giggling through the years.

Beneath a blanket of luminescent white,
There are games of charades, take a bite!
With seals and foxes in raucous debate,
Over who has the best wintertime fate.

In this frosty realm, where laughter's the game,
With each icy joke, you'll never feel lame.
So listen close to the calls from the site,
In the vastness of winter, find joy in the night!

Frostbitten Melodies of the Deep

Fish in tuxedos, waltzing afloat,
Claiming the crown of the icy moat.
They giggle and dance in a frosty parade,
While seaweed confetti is whimsically made.

A seal with a hat tells a joke to a shrimp,
Laughter erupts as they ballroom and primp.
An octopus juggles with squishy delight,
While bubbles of laughter rise up to the night.

Penguins slide by, tripping in style,
They tumble and laugh, all in good while.
Snowflakes are giggling, the breeze gives a tease,
In a world of their own, they do what they please.

Under the surface, the fun never halts,
With every splash, there's a chuckle that vaults.
In this frozen realm where joy intricately creeps,
The melodies shimmer, and the laughter leaps.

Resonance of a Shattered Silence

Bubbles are popping, it's quite a charade,
Crabs in a conga dance, perfectly swayed.
Whales are composing some tunes of delight,
As seals take requests in the coldness of night.

An icy bear played the drum on a floe,
Made music from snowflakes that began to blow.
Hilarity strikes like a shock from the past,
As penguins together hold off a snow blast.

Fish that wear glasses are keeping the beat,
While flopping around in their frosty retreat.
Each frozen note sparkles, white glimmers of fun,
In the winter wonder, they sing till they're done.

With laughter as thick as a snow-covered plank,
Creatures all gather, it's all they can thank.
In giddy bemusement, they celebrate cheer,
In a frozen dimension where joy's ever near.

Beneath the Veil of Winter's Breath

A walrus wears shades, reclining on ice,
While seals look on, thinking it's quite nice.
They sip on hot cocoa through straws made of kelp,
In the frozen café, where they chuckle and yelp.

Frosted cupcakes adorn every fin's make,
As polar bears bake up a sweet winter cake.
They slip in the kitchen, a floury mess,
Prancing in giggles, they truly impress.

An icy igloo filled with laughter and noise,
Where snowballs are flying, oh such silly joys.
Turtles on skates are doing a glide,
With snickers and snorts, they can't help but slide.

Beneath all this frost, there's warmth in the mirth,
Laughter reverberates, a gift of the earth.
In this chilly ballet, where nonsense is rife,
Every creature partakes in the sweetness of life.

The Call of the Icy Hollow

In the hollow of ice, where the funny stuff's seen,
Otters wear hats and waltz with a bean.
A jolly old walrus hums tunes from the sea,
While squirrels in tuxedos dance happily free.

In the frosty abyss, a grand party unfurls,
Bears break the dance floor, giving twirls.
They spin with such vigor, a frosty ballet,
As laughs roll like thunder, come join in the play.

Snowflakes as confetti rain down with a splash,
Polar bears giggle, their antics a smash.
With every light-hearted flutter of snow,
A symphony rises in this winter-show.

When midnight strikes, and laughter sings clear,
The critters unite, with love and good cheer.
This hollow of ice, a comedic delight,
Is where all the creatures find joy in the night.

Reverberating in the Lamblike Calm

A sheep on the pond, quite daft,
Slips on a patch with a laugh!
It bounces back, round and round,
Woolly chaos on frozen ground.

Beneath the surface, fish hold their breath,
Wondering if the ice is life or death.
But wait! Here comes a bumbling hare,
Dancing with flair without a care.

The sun peeks out, ice starts to crack,
A troupe of squirrels, ready to attack!
They dash and weave in a goofy spree,
While ducks are just watching in glee.

With each slip and tumble, giggles ensue,
Nature's own circus, with laughter so true!
In the lamblike calm, silliness thrives,
While nature chuckles, and hilarity jives.

Silent Ballet of the Frozen Waters

The penguins in tuxes, oh what a sight,
Twirl and they tumble, with all of their might.
Slipping and sliding, they take center stage,
In a silent ballet, they earn a new wage.

Fish bulge their eyes, incredulous and wide,
As the penguins pirouette, full of pride.
An audience formed by the curious seals,
Who clap their flippers, sharing their meals.

A polar bear joins, all grace lost in dance,
He tumbles around, not missing a chance.
With a comical flair, he takes his grand bow,
On stage made of ice, he looks like a cow.

Yet as the curtain falls, so chilly yet bright,
The frozen ballet fades into night.
Laughter and frolics fill all of the air,
The silent stage holds memories rare.

Fragments of Time in Crystal Silence

Icicles hanging like odd silver teeth,
A squirrel spins tales of winter beneath.
Tick-tock goes time in this frosty arc,
Now chilly and bright, now a comforting dark.

A deer with a beard made of icy fluff,
Looks like he's had quite enough!
He twirls 'round a tree, chuckling out loud,
While snowflakes fall and form a strange crowd.

Old frostbitten gossip drifts through the air,
As snowmen hold court without a care.
They plot their escape as the sun starts to rise,
Knowing that warmth means some chilly goodbyes.

Yet in this freeze, joy lingers on near,
As laughter ricochets off each frozen sphere.
Fragments of laughter, frozen, we find,
In crystal silence, warmth is entwined.

Glacial Whispers of the Past

Snowflakes giggle as they drift down,
Wrestling with breezes, they wear a light crown.
A bear trying yoga thinks he's a swan,
But his belly flop makes the giggles go on.

Memories swirl like a frosty white dance,
As ancient trees join in with a prance.
Reshaping old stories with a wink and a shout,
The frozen wind whispers laughter about.

Beneath all the layers, a turtle hums tunes,
While ice cream cones freeze under bright moons.
Fortunes foretold in the flicker of light,
All in good fun on this magical night.

So here's to the giggles beneath all the frost,
In glacial whispers, not a moment is lost.
Silliness wrapped in the chill of the scene,
With laughter aplenty, the past reigns serene.